The Belligerent Finisher

The
Belligerent
Finisher

John Porritt

Lost Art
PRESS

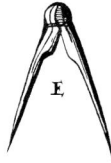

Published by Lost Art Press LLC in 2022
837 Willard St., Covington, KY 41011, USA
Web: http://lostartpress.com

Title: The Belligerent Finisher
Author: John Porritt
Copyright ©2022 John Porritt
Publisher: Christopher Schwarz
Editor: Megan Fitzpatrick
Distribution: John Hoffman
Cover photos: Lydia Curran

ISBN: 978-1-954697-09-6

First printing.

This book was printed and bound in the United States.
Signature Book Printing, Inc.
http://signature-book.com

Contents

Acknowledgments

With grateful thanks to the restorers Spike Knight, John Gould and John Bellinger, who have helped and inspired me in so many ways; to Scott Mesick for his woodworking knowledge and wood supply; to Tom Curran and Lydia Curran. And to John Whiteley for being there. Without our editor Megan Fitzpatrick's help and patience, this would've gone on forever. Thank you so much.

My gratitude goes to stellar chairmakers John Brown, Chris Schwarz and Chris Williams. Without their encouragement this book would not exist. Tim Bowen of Ferryside, Wales, was the catalyst of our fortuitous meeting. Who knew that a few of my chair pictures falling out of a book in Wales would lead to this.

To all my friends and loved ones who have encouraged and helped me along the way – thank you.

In Memoriam: Keith Rand, 1956–2013, sculptor and chairmaker. The best.

Dedicated to Sue & Mia

A comb-back chair I built that was finished using the techniques in this book.

Why Add Age to a Chair?

In addition to the finish, texture and toolmarks are important to creating a chair with a magical old quality.

I have always loved pieces of country furniture that have come out of the hills – objects that have been touched by time with all its nuances but have never been cleaned or worked over. To my eye some of these pieces can possess a beauty not yet attained in a new, unfinished piece or one left with a simple paint, oil or wax finish.

Living in America, feeling somewhat cut off in the midst of the 2020-2022 pandemic, I found myself remembering and missing some of the things from the borderland of England and Wales, where I had my home. The light on the hills, the glorious landscape, the characters at the Welshpool Friday market. And then Ian Anderson's antique shop: there I would see, touch and enjoy some of the pieces he had bought at auction or come across by invitation

Multiple layers of finish and wear create a believable surface.

throughout Mid Wales. Form, color and surface – he found some delightful things. I missed the joy of the old oak dressers, the tables and chairs with their marvelous well-worn surfaces. That is why I started playing with my chair finishes, to get some of that feeling into my newly made chairs. You see, I have no interest in making fake antiques. Instead, with my finishing techniques I strive to create chairs that I want to see, chairs that I cannot find or even if they were about, chairs that I couldn't begin to afford.

This book will take you through the steps and techniques I have used in my work as a chairmaker, and furniture and tool restorer, to simulate the textures, colors and the mellow glow that is prized in old work. It requires simple tools, such as a deer antler I found on a walk, some stones I picked up from a beach walk in Rhode Island and a chainmail burnisher/pot scrubber. Plus, some chemicals – some relatively harmless (cement dust) and some that require great caution (nitric acid).

These finishes also require a bit of "belligerence." And by that, I mean mostly perseverance. Creating these finishes requires you to apply finish, wipe it off, burnish it, heat it or even gently burn it off (I definitely do not mean char it). Then stop to take a look at your progress. You may have to do it all again (and again) until all the parts of your chair are to your liking, and you have created a believable surface.

Like restoring furniture surfaces, this process is about "play" – working and reworking a surface until you get the desired result.

Should you feel somewhat nervous piling in with these techniques on a new chair, practice on small boards, chair legs and spindles. Using different woods, take notes of the effects you have come across and build yourself a parts library to refer to.

I do think these finishes are worth the work. I find that they inspire me and lift my spirits.

Safety Note: Like everything in life, safety is your responsibility. All the techniques shown in this book can be executed safely if you take the right precautions with protective gear and work in a well-ventilated shop. Read and obey the safety notices printed on all the finishing materials you use (or consult the product's "safety data sheet" online for full details). Know and understand your finishing materials before mixing them or applying them.

Work in a well-ventilated area. Read and understand all the warnings and hazards associated with the chemicals and tools you are using.

Two arms waiting to hold you. Left, ash; right, hickory. Both seats are white oak.

Tools for Adding Age

The nylon brush that I chuck into my hand drill.

The following tools are ones you might not have on hand in your wood-working shop. Most of them are inexpensive and easy to obtain.

Nylon Wire Brush Drum. This drum, which measures 4-1/2" x 4-3/4", chucks into my handheld drill with the help of a 3/4" steel shaft (sold separately). Made by Black Hawk Abrasives, the drum is designed to remove scale and rust from metal. But I use it to provide texture. The nylon bristles remove some of the softer earlywood to simulate years of wear.

Many antique restorers use these tools to simulate age, especially on the secondary woods in a piece of furniture. I use the brush mostly on the sitting area of a chair – where the body meets the wood – to simulate wear.

I suspect a brass- or steel-bristle hand brush would work as well.

Propane Torch. The torch can be used for everything from lightly and carefully burning off the small fuzzies that appear after raising the grain, to burning off alcohol I've wiped on the chair's components.

Combining fire with flammable finishing materials requires great care. Work in a well-ventilated shop, always have a fire extinguisher handy and practice on test pieces before you start torching your chair's components.

Heat Gun. Typically used for removing paint, a heat gun is handy to have to speed along the drying time of finishes, water or other material applied to a chair. Sometimes I use the heat gun to alter a finish.

Chainmail Burnisher/Pot Scrubber. This common handheld cleaning tool is ideal for burnishing surfaces – compressing the finish and wood beneath – without scratching the material. The tool can also help bring up a mellow shine on dull surfaces. The one I have is from the early 20th century; today they are typically made from stainless steel, so they are easily cleaned of finishing materials.

Antlers. I use a couple of deer antlers as a burnishing tool. They are more aggressive than the pot scrubber. And I can bear down on certain areas – such as the front edge of a chair or the tops of tenons – to create a surface that will refract light and look like it has been used. If you cannot get deer antlers, a slightly bent screwdriver with a smooth shaft can also work. Also, a piece of harder wood than your work – shaped to suit the job in hand – can work well.

Brass-bristle Brush. These small brushes are ideal for distressing paint. They can pull paint out of open-pored wood, such as oak. They're also useful to simulate gentle scuffing. I use my father's old suede brush with a 2" head.

A commercial heat gun helps speed the drying time of chemicals and finishes.

A chainmail burnisher is one of the primary tools I use to alter the chair surface.

Deer antlers are excellent tools for consolidating and burnishing material.

Heavy chain links, used sparingly, add realistic small dents.

Links of Heavy Chain (various sizes). Used with a cotton cloth, to visually soften the indentations made, these short bits of chain make small dents on surfaces to mimic wear. Many amateur finishers overdo it with the chain. Used properly, the effect is subtle and believable.

Small Smooth Rocks. A handful of small rocks can also provide small dents and areas of wear on a seat. Like the chain, these should be used gently to create a realistic effect.

These small smooth rocks add further small dents to the high-wear areas of a chair.

Chip Brushes. For some finishing operations, I will use my natural-bristle brushes. But for most of these processes, inexpensive chip brushes are ideal. They don't require much care, and if they get too gunked up, you can replace them. I've found a fair few at tag sales.

Paper Towels. Household paper towels are ideal for rubbing away a semi-dry finish to create the illusion that a layer of paint or other finish has been worn away. Paper towels will remove part of the finish without burnishing the surface.

Huck Towels. These towels – typically used in hospitals and in car care – are a special weave that prevents them from leaving strings behind. The towels are slightly coarse, so they are ideal for burnishing a waxed surface and can be more aggressive than a paper towel.

3M Non-Woven Abrasive Pad (Gray). These pads and a little alcohol are ideal for evening out the boundary between a painted surface and an adjacent worn surface.

Nitric acid, even highly diluted, is nasty stuff. So take care.

Chemicals

When working with chemicals, be sure to take proper safety precautions, and work in a well-ventilated area.

Nitric Acid. Nitric acid is a corrosive mineral acid that I use (greatly watered down) to simulate the beginning of an oxidized surface. You can purchase it from chemical supply companies (where it typically has been watered down to some degree). And then dilute it more in your shop. Typically I dilute the purchased acid 20 parts water to one part acid. Also, this is VERY important: Always add the acid to the water, not the other way around.

A Solution of Vinegar and Iron. This mixture will darken the wood. I usually make the mixture a week ahead of time by putting a pad of Liberon oil-free steel wool into a glass jar of white vinegar. The vinegar will dissolve the steel wool, creating a dyeing solution.

Mahogany Oil Stain. You'll need a quality oil stain in a brown mahogany color. I use W.S. Jenkins (a U.K. brand from Tottenham, London) and have stuck with it even though I now live in the States. I encourage you to experiment with oil stains that are readily available to you and find a favorite.

Washing Soda. This neutralizes the nitric acid. I use Arm & Hammer Laundry Booster, which I mix two flat tablespoons to one pint of water, worked into the surface to be neutralized. Then liberally rinse with water.

Hydrogen Peroxide. This chemical is widely available at any drugstore. I apply it to the chair after the nitric acid and before the washing soda. The hydrogen peroxide will reduce the red should you find it too fierce. You may need to do this two or three times. Neutralize with white vinegar (a weak acetic acid).

Black Milk Paint. The black chair in Chapter 1 was painted using a milk paint I made myself. The pigment is one that I acquired in England many years ago and I'm not sure now exactly what it is. I do remember it came from Gedge's in Shoreditch, London, before it closed down. I have recently experimented with Arabian Night by The Real Milk Paint Co. It's good — more of a gray, gunmetal black. If you want a dense black similar to the historic chairs, I would suggest you make your own, staying away from the blue blacks in order to replicate the look of the past. Should you wish to make your own milk paint, I suggest using a ratio of 5 parts milk powder to 2 parts lime, then adding black pigment to get a saturated black. Kremer Pigments in New York City offers black pigments.

Green Milk Paint (commercial). For one of the chairs, I have used Lily Pad green from The Real Milk Paint Co. You can choose any color you like. I do mix it thicker than the directions recommend, like a slightly runny yogurt.

Khaki Wax & Antique Wax. This khaki wax is ideal for aging chairs as it won't appear as white when it gets into the pores of the wood. The antique wax is a much darker brown and is a good all-around color. I use Harrell's wax polish made by W.S. Jenkins of Tottenham, London. This wax is available in the U.S. I'm sure other brands would work.

Tannic Tea. This homemade tea solution adds tannins to woods that are not naturally tannic, such as elm. I first make a strong black tea and let the tea steep overnight. Then I add a little household ammonia so the resulting mixture is one part ammonia to nine parts tea.

Denatured Alcohol. This is widely available at any hardware store. Note that some brands have less methanol, so they are less toxic.

Seedlac. Any dark shellac will work well, however I do avoid garnet and other red shellacs. I favor seedlac because it mimics the look of the past. Seedlac is available at shellac.net. I mix my own, then strain it once through muslin.

Boiled Linseed Oil. Available at any hardware store.

Portland Cement. Typically used in masonry, this cement is used to add crustiness to an aged finish. You can purchase it at any home center or quality hardware store. (With thanks to John Bellinger for this helpful tip.)

Stippling more green paint around the tenons.

In the white, chairs look much bigger than they do once they have color added. You can see how the finished chairs look much smaller than the raw backstool.

One coat of nitric acid (and a little heat), and the chair already begins to look more in scale with the chairs behind it.

With the finishing complete, the appearance of wear is believable along the seat, sticks and comb.

The Black Chair: Backstool No. 1

The goal with this chair is to create a finish that is black paint that has been worn through over the years to expose the wood beneath, which has reddened over time. I built this chair using white elm and ash, plus one stick that is hickory, a common feature of old country chairs. When I see this in old chairs I think that perhaps the chair was made that way because of the wood that was on hand, or perhaps the hickory stick was a repair after one of the original sticks broke.

When I build a chair such as this, I avoid using sandpaper. All of the chair's surfaces are straight from the tool – shaves, planes, saws, rasps and scrapers, which lends a clarity to the finished article. If you use sandpaper, the scratches can show in the finished piece as a slight amorphous bloom.

I also leave my leg tenons a little proud of the seat, plus any small pegs that I used to secure tenons in the chair. In most old chairs, the tenons have become proud from the chair being used, and these tenons will be burnished during the finishing process to add to the realism of the work.

Surface Preparation. I begin by burning off any wispy bits of stray wood with a blowtorch, quickly going over the entire chair. Then I wipe down all surfaces with a heavy coat of water and dry it off with a heat gun. Finally, I chuck a nylon brush drum into a drill and go over the chair briefly to begin the wear process.

Apply the Nitric Acid. Nitric acid is one of the nastiest chemicals I use in finishing, and it must be handled with the utmost care. It is available from most chemical supply houses. Usually it comes thinned with water. And I dilute it significantly more: 1 part acid to 20 parts water. Always add the acid to the water – never the other way around. Also, be sure to keep a bucket of water around. In case you spill the acid, pour water on the spill to dilute it.

The acid will begin the process of aging - oxidizing the bare wood. Initially it will be somewhat orange. This will be muted as we continue the process. Unlike when using a stain, which can muddy the wood, the acid will allow the clarity of the wood to remain. Because the acid reacts with the wood, it won't be removed or wiped off when burnishing it later on.

Begin brushing the acid on one part of the chair, using a chip brush. Wait a minute and then chase with the heat gun on high heat. Observe the color. If

A quick pass over the chair with a small propane torch will remove any stray wispies from the construction process.

it looks good, continue the process evenly over the entire chair. After the acid has dried it can be neutralized with a mixture of washing soda – two table-spoons to a pint of water works well. Brush it on, work it in, then rinse it off with cold water, checking that you haven't left any white crystals of washing soda in the grain. Do all of the above thoroughly.

I cannot stress enough how necessary it is to observe all safety protocols when working this way. This method of coloring is an art, not a science – so

To test the strength of the acid, apply the nitric acid with a chip brush to a small area, such as the comb.

the need is to be flexible and very aware. It does make sense to practice and experiment on small pieces as you grow your skills and experience. At all times wear the appropriate gloves, mask, protective clothing and eyewear, making sure to be working in a well ventilated area.

To clarify: Chase the acid with a hot air gun. If it is too strong, wait about half an hour – it can lighten. If it hasn't, give it two coats of hydrogen peroxide, chase it with a hot air gun and reassess. If this looks good, neutralize with

Then use a heat gun to bring out the orange color from the acid. Adjust the mixture of the acid if necessary.

white vinegar. Should the strength of color persist, you can give it a coat of warm oxalic acid. This can then be cleaned first with warm soapy water, then rinsed with cold water. Should you find areas that haven't taken the color, you may have used far too weak a mix, put it on too sparingly or – the most likely – you may have left glue on the surface. Clean and/or scrape it off and do it again.

If any areas fail to react to the acid, try scraping those areas and apply acid and heat again.

Now apply acid on the entire chair.

Then use the heat gun to add the orange to the remainder of the acid-coated surfaces.

Washing soda dissolved in water neutralizes the acid. If you see a lot of crystals form, you can wash these off with a scrub brush and water.

Wipe the chair down with a 3-percent hydrogen peroxide solution to cut the orange back a little bit.

After the coat of hydrogen peroxide, dry it with the heat gun.

Burnishing. With the first color complete, now I begin to burnish the surfaces of the chair to compress the wood in areas where it would see wear. I begin by burnishing the front edge of the seat and the tops of the tenons with a deer antler. The antler will make surfaces that refract light and make it look as if the chair has seen significant use. Then I'll move on to burnishing the rim of the seat, rounding over its sharp corners. And then the front surface and top edges of the chair's comb.

After burnishing these surfaces with the antler, I work the tenons with the rounded end of an old screwdriver to further shape them.

Then I switch to the chainmail burnisher and work between the sticks. The chainmail burnisher is less aggressive than the antler. I then work on the sticks, legs and the comb with the chainmail burnisher, but I take it easy on the chair's secondary surfaces.

Burnishing is important because it acts as a base for the wax that is added later on. If you add wax without burnishing, the surface will look flat and lifeless.

Use a deer antler to burnish the areas that should look worn, especially the front edge of the seat, the tops of the tenons and the comb.

Burnishing is quite physical. It begins to compress the wood, bringing out tool marks and other imperfections, preparing it for the final waxing.

A chainmail burnisher gets between the sticks to burnish and mark the areas that have less contact with the sitter.

As I work on the chair, it's usually on my workbench. But when I want to evaluate my work, I always place the chair on the floor of the workshop. All the shine will appear to be on top, with no depth of surface. That gives me a more realistic view of how my work is going.

Black Milk Paint. For the top coat of the chair, I mix up a black milk paint. The recipe is approximately 5 parts milk powder to 2 parts lime, and a couple of good tablespoons of black pigment to create a mixture just shy of a sludge. You could also use Arabian Night milk paint from The Real Milk Paint Co. – it looks good to me.

Apply the milk paint over the chair in sections with a large artist's brush. Begin with the comb. While the paint is still wet, use a wet rag or a wet paper towel to remove the paint in the wear areas of that part, such as the middle of the comb.

When you paint the sticks, apply an extra-heavy coat of paint, as if it were done quickly. On the seat, remove a good deal of paint from the front half of the seat, leaving a lot of paint around the sticks. On the legs, be sure to remove a lot of paint from the bottoms of the legs – these areas see a lot of wear.

On areas of the chair that don't see a lot of wear, such as the stretchers, let the paint set up a while before rubbing them with a towel.

Once the paint is dry, burnish the chair with the chainmail burnisher to mark up the paint.

After studying the seat, I usually paint in some more black in the transition between its painted area and worn-through area, blending the transition between the two areas by working back and forth between a paint brush and a wet paper towel.

When that looks good, I return to burnishing the front edge of the seat and its tenons with the deer antler. And I'll burnish the entire chair a little more with a chainmail burnisher for good measure.

Add enough water to the milk paint mixture to make a thick-bodied paint – almost a sludge.

Apply a healthy coat of the black milk paint with an artist's brush. While the paint is still wet, wipe away the paint from the high-wear areas using a wet rag or paper towel.

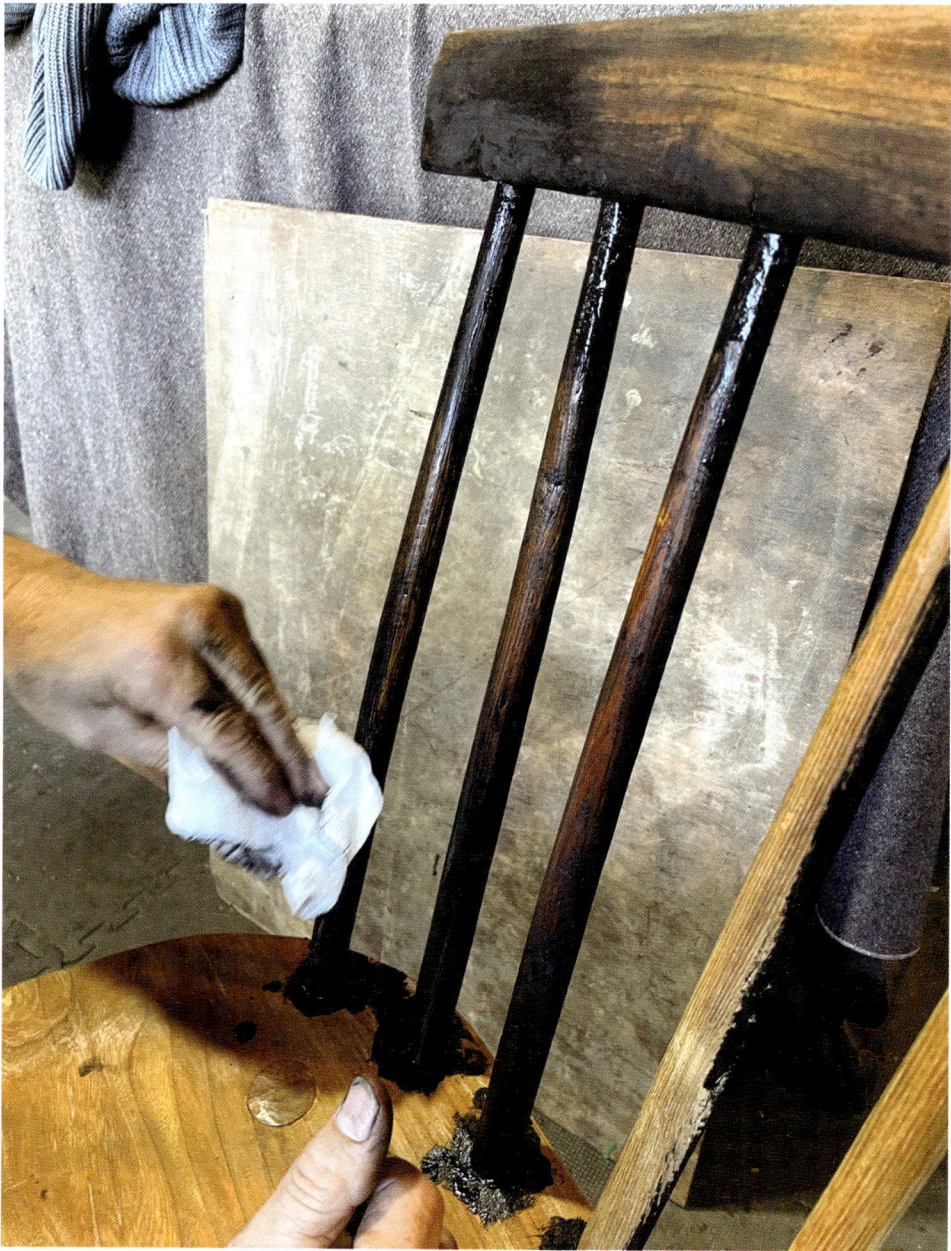

The sticks get a very heavy coat of paint, which will lend them lots of personality in the finished chair.

The seat must look convincing. Begin by wiping the front part of the seat. You will blend these two colors shortly.

The bottoms of the legs are wiped vigorously to remove a good deal of the paint. The stretchers are rubbed only after the paint has set up a bit.

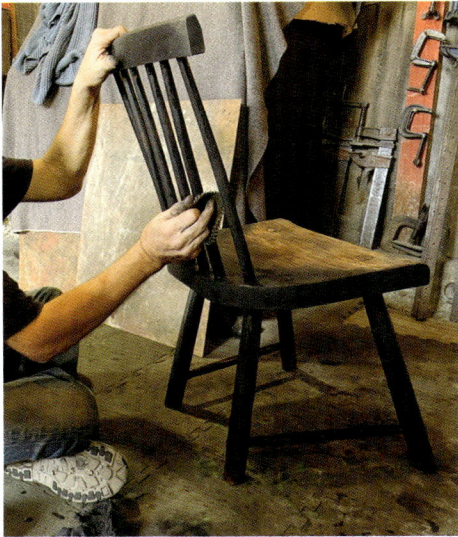

After wiping away some of the paint, continue the aging process by going over the surfaces with a chainmail burnisher, particularly the bottoms of the legs.

Work the transition between the black and orange areas of the seat. Add some more paint, then daub it with a wet paper towel to refine the seat's appearance.

When the paint dries, burnish the wear areas again with your antler and your chainmail burnisher. This dry surface can be attractive – some prefer it to a waxed finish. If this is the look you like, you can finish it by rubbing the area of wear with a cloth that has been lightly used to take wax off. Do this sparingly to gain a soft glow.

Waxing. Waxing is what gives the chair a warm glow. For most of the chair I use Harrell's W010 khaki wax. I prefer khaki wax because a white wax will show in the pores as white flecks. Because the legs see so much wear, I use a black wax down there. Then buff out the wax with a soft cloth.

After aging a chair, be sure to let the colors mellow before you decide to make any changes. These chairs get better with time. And the best way to start the process is by the workshop stove with a good cup of tea.

A coat of khaki wax adds a warm glow to the chair and helps unify all the surfaces.

While similar to its cousin behind it, this chair features a square-cornered seat and a backrest that is straight. Soon, many of these crisp lines will be eased by burnishing.

With the finishing complete, the appearance of wear is believable along the seat, sticks and comb.

The Green Chair: Backstool No. 2

This second side chair is made of oak. The seat is white oak and the rest of its parts are red oak. Because I built this chair using American species, the grain is quite straight and regular. With Welsh stick chairs and other vernacular forms, the wood is often quite gnarly. So my goal with this chair is to add quite a bit of texture to make the chair more interesting.

To help the chair look more like an old survivor, I used young, small-diameter trees. These were available to me after the workers came through. Now they're all using wood chippers, which is most unfortunate – certainly for me. The grain of these small trees has more character than large-diameter trees with long-straight trunks.

In addition to the texture, I want the chair to have a nice chestnut brown color to the wood that looks like it has been covered in green paint – a common color on old chairs. In the areas where the sitter would rub against the seat, the green paint will be worn through. Plus, like all chairs that have had a long and interesting life, this chair will have lots of burnished surfaces.

Just like with the first chair, this chair was finished straight from the tools – no sandpaper. Plus the tenons and any pegs have been left a little proud, which makes them easy to burnish.

Surface Preparation. I begin this process by giving the chair a good soaking with water, which will raise the grain and soften it. I immediately follow that with the nylon brush, which is chucked into an electric drill. This is the first step to adding texture, as the nylon bristles wear away some of the softer earlywood in the oak.

You could probably get the same effect with a wire brush. As you go over your chair, spend more time brushing the areas that would contact the sitter, including the seat, sticks, backrest and the leg ends.

It may seem strange to hear about using the nylon wheel brush to take out the soft earlywood and then burnish it to get a surface skin. The thing with old surfaces is they have undulations. Sometimes these are like a fine ripple, a movement to the surface where the wood has shrunk, expanded with moisture, or been abraded by time so that there are ridges and troughs. It's not a surface straight from a cutting tool, so the brush action gets movement into the wood and the burnishing pulls it over to consolidate it. A good, used, worn surface that reflects light in an uneven fashion.

Give the piece a good soaking with water to raise the grain and soften the wood a bit.

The nylon brush adds texture to the piece by gently wearing away some of the softer earlywood. Focus your efforts on the areas that contact the sitter.

Add Color. Before I start adding color to a piece, I'll make sample sticks using scraps from the project itself. This prevents unwanted surprises.

The first coloring step requires us to first add tannin to the wood. Then we'll add a solution made with vinegar and steel wool, which reacts with the tannins to give a nice, aged color to the wood.

To make the tannic solution, first make a batch of strong, black tea that you steep overnight (do not add milk or sugar). With the tea at room temperature, add some household ammonia – the final mixture should be about 10 percent ammonia and 90 percent tea. (Use ammonia without added soap.)

Sample sticks are a roadmap for your finishing process and show you how the different colors and chemicals will interact. It can be helpful to label each sample.

The ammonia seems to help drive the tannins into the wood.

Once the mixture is applied, I follow that by going over all the surfaces with a heat gun. The heat gun raises the grain and speeds the process along. If you aren't in a hurry, you can let the tea flash off on its own.

Now it's time to add the color. The solution is made by dissolving a pad of oil-free steel wool in a jar of household white vinegar. I make mine in a large lidded jar. It usually takes three days to a week for the metal to dissolve. I also like to make batches in different strengths. You can make a stronger color by adding more steel wool to the solution.

I brush the solution on with a chip brush. If the wood does not quickly turn a brown/black, you should use a stronger solution. Set the chair aside and allow the solution to dry.

Add tannins to the wood by brushing on a solution of black tea mixed with household ammonia.

You can let the tea dry on its own schedule or speed the process along with a heat gun.

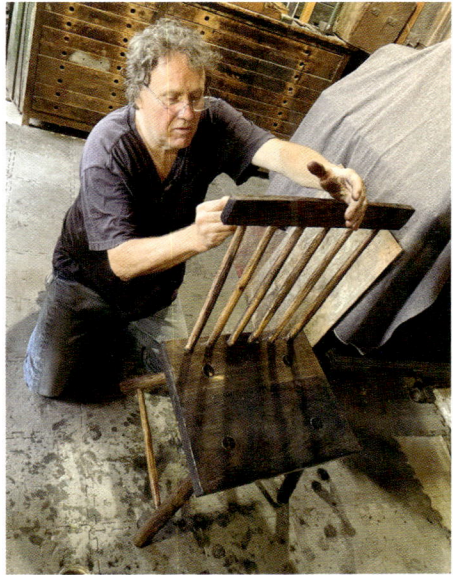

The vinegar and iron solution should turn the wood a blackish color. If no color appears – or it is weak – use a stronger solution.

Burnishing. Burnishing a piece is just as important and time-consuming as adding color. I begin burnishing the front edge of the seat with a smooth deer antler. Firm pressure compresses the wood fibers so that they will reflect light. I also use the antler on the sharp corners of the seat, on top of the tenons and on the backrest.

The small, pointy end of the antler can get in places the broad middle section cannot.

I follow the antler with the chainmail burnisher, again paying most of my attention to the places that will contact the sitter and the legs of the chair.

Then I take a small hammer and gently tap the sharp corners of the seat and the backrest, rounding them.

A smooth deer antler compresses the wood at the front of the seat, on the tops of the tenons and on the backrest. Use firm downward pressure.

Follow up the antler by burnishing the chair with the chainmail burnisher.

Oil Stain. The next step is to add a coat of a brown mahogany oil stain (I use W.S. Jenkins in the U.K.). I'm trying to get a really nice oaky color, so I apply the oil stain quite thick with a brush. The goal is to get the wood as dark as I can. Welsh oak can get really dark, with a reddish chestnut color coming through the black.

Apply the oil stain with a brush. After it has dried for a moment, you can manipulate the color with a paper towel.

Finishing is all about building color and then taking some off. Building again and taking some off. Again and again until it looks right. There is no "one-can" finish out there that looks good. So our next step is to let the stain dry for about a minute and then wipe off the excess with a rag. To my eye, this tends to even the color out.

After the stain dries, I manipulate it some more with alcohol and fire. I rub the chair with a thin coat of denatured alcohol in the wear areas and then carefully light the alcohol with a lighter or the propane torch. I'll repeat this a few times on the seat, plus the front of the sticks and the backrest. This will pull some of the color out. It sounds odd, but some even non-evenness is required. Perhaps a better explanation would be not too uniform.

Wipe off the excess with a paper towel or rag. This step will help even out the color on the chair.

The last step with the oil stain is to wipe some denatured alcohol onto the heavy-wear areas. Then light it with a propane torch.

Green Milk Paint. I like to use milk paint that is thicker than usual. The milk paint for this chair was the thickness of typical latex – not a watery wash. A thicker-bodied paint is easier to manipulate and remove. I like the Lily Pad green color from The Real Milk Paint Co., which is what I'm using here. But your taste might be different.

Add water to the powder, shake it up and let the paint sit for 30 minutes or so. Then add water or powder until you get to the viscosity you desire.

Apply the paint with a pure bristle brush. Before the paint dries, it's back to manipulating the color. Use a paper towel that is moistened with water to wipe the wear areas of the chair to remove some of the paint, especially the feet, the seat and the backrest. Now take the chainmail burnisher and mark

Mix the milk paint so it is the viscosity of latex paint. This will coat the chair better and is easier to manipulate.

the paint with the tool. You aren't trying to heavily burnish the surface – just dent and scratch the paint.

After wiping with the paper towel, I return to wiping on a thin coat of alcohol on wear areas and burning it off with a torch. Then more burnishing with the chainmail burnisher. I'll even use a brass-bristle brush to distress the wear areas, using it to pull paint out of the wood's pores if need be.

The lower legs of the chair need special attention at this point. Because the legs see a lot of scuffing, I wipe paint thinner on the legs. I'll wipe hard at the feet and ease up the pressure as I move up the leg.

The last step with the paint is to dab it in the transitions between the brown stain and green paint to make the wear look believable.

Even though a fair amount of paint will be rubbed away, paint the entire chair.

While the paint is still wet, use a paper towel to wipe away paint from the areas that would see heavy wear. Then mark the paint using a chainmail burnisher.

Then apply alcohol to the wear areas and ignite it immediately with a propane torch. Follow this up with some burnishing with the chainmail burnisher.

Dab the area where the green paint gives way to the colors below. Managing this transition is important to make the wear look believable.

Shellac & Oil. With the paint dry, I'll add a coat of seedlac shellac and then burn it off. The idea is not to get rid of the shellac but crystallize it – take some of the shine out of it. This dark shellac doesn't have to be high quality. After I brush the shellac on the seat, I'll torch the seat before the alcohol flashes off. Then I move onto the sticks, the backrest and then the undercarriage of the chair, brushing and burning each section before the alcohol dries off.

The charred shellac adds a crystalline quality to the surface finish, which you see on old pieces.

Next I apply a mixture of Portland cement and boiled linseed oil, and lock it in with a heat gun. The Portland cement will give the finish a crusty look. After painting on a coat of oil, I sprinkle some cement in some of the areas that should look dirty, especially between the sticks and around the tenons.

Then I hit the oil finish with a heat gun and a carefully used blowtorch to dry it. Like a lot of the steps in this finishing process, there is a lot of looking, adding more oil, removing some excess, applying heat, burnishing and looking to see the result.

To give the finish a crusty look, apply a good coat of seedlac to a component and then immediately burn it with a torch. Take great care with this.

A coat of boiled linseed oil and Portland cement add color and texture to the chair's surfaces. While the oil is wet, very carefully torch the surfaces.

Dents & Waxing. To add some age, I turn to a cloth and heavy chain links. I know the hackneyed stories of antique fakers beating a piece with a chain, but that's not what we're going to do here. Instead, I cover the seat with a cloth and then move the chain around on the cloth. I'm looking for soft dents, which are cushioned by the cloth.

After the chain, I burnish the finish with the chainmail burnisher. Then I repeat the process: heavy chains on a cloth followed by burnishing with the chainmail burnisher. Stand back, look at your work and figure out your next step.

When you are happy with the dents and burnishing, the chair needs a coat of wax. I use Harrell's antique wax polish (W009) mixed with a little roof cement to get the right color and consistency, using approximately 90 percent wax, to 10 percent roofing cement. This is a technique I learned from Dan Faia.

The wax and roof cement mixture adds some shine to the chair, and it also leaves a slight dirtiness in the cracks and crevices. I add a thick coat of wax all over the chair (except the underside of the seat) and let it sit for about 40 minutes so the mixture will not come off easily.

I rub out the wax with a coarse huck-weave towel. Then I burnish the wax all over the chair with the chainmail burnisher. This will burnish the grain to make the wood's texture more apparent. At this stage I frequently put the chair on the floor and walk around it to see what it looks like. Then on to some more burnishing.

Adding subtle bumps and dents to the chair adds to the overall finish. This is easy to overdo. Use a soft cloth between the chair and a heavy chain. Simply move the chain around; you don't want to beat the chair.

Apply a thick coat of furniture wax mixed with a little roofing cement. Then let the wax set up for 40 minutes.

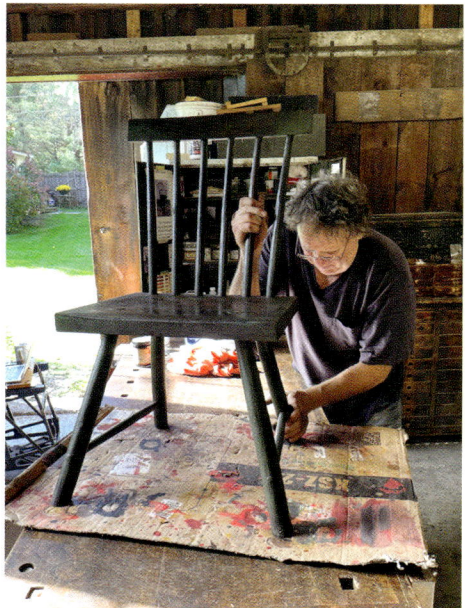

Use a coarse towel to buff out the wax. Then follow this up with some burnishing with the chainmail burnisher.

Here you can see the net effect of the labor. Note the realistic gunk around the base of the sticks and the burnished tenons.

Finish the Finish. The last little bits involve a little back and forth. I wipe on some alcohol using a 3M gray pad and set it on fire to spirit off the wax. Then I might rub the finish with a towel soaked with alcohol. Then some more alcohol and more burning.

The last step involves the seat. I wipe on a coat of the wax/roofing cement mixture on the seat, then I buff it off almost immediately. Then I put a little more around the tenons and rub that out almost immediately.

Lastly, I get some small rocks I found on a beach and scatter them on the seat. I move them around with a soft cloth so they gently mark the surface finish.

To finish up the seat, apply some alcohol and immediately burn it off. Then apply a coat of the wax/roofing cement mixture and immediately buff that out.

A last bit of texture. Use a soft cloth to push around some small rocks scattered on the seat.

Gallery of Chairs

Left: the "hands" of two chairs. Above: A scarf joint on one of the armbows of my chairs. The details of the finish are extremely important to me.

I think the phrase "standing on the shoulders of giants" has the ring of truth, certainly in woodworking. That, and the idiosyncratic nature of many vernacular woodworkers, plus the vagaries of time, have inspired me to try to understand some of the mystery of the old stick chairs. To work with that, simulate it (or "stimulate" as my old friend Johnny Jones would have said) and then, on occasion – having fallen short – sitting down in an odd chair with a restorative cup of tea, to ponder having another go. That's my form of belligerence, and these are some of my chairs.

My first Welsh-inspired stick chair, made circa 1994 in Shropshire, England. I sent photos of several English and American-influenced chairs along with one of this chair – which draws on what at the time I thought of as a Welsh stick chair – to John Brown. He kindly wrote back to me and for a while we had a correspondence. He went so far as to speak highly of the chair and published a photo in *Good Woodworking* magazine. Looking back I now feel this chair is an amalgam of John Brown's work with the steam-bent arm and an American way of shaping the hands, along with an exaggerated Welsh comb. It was my jumping-off point as I started to look more carefully at what the old Welsh chairmakers, in all their diversity, had achieved.

The chair has lived in Shropshire ever since and is a well-used and appreciated member of a friend's family. It has an elm seat and steam-bent ash arm-bow, with ash legs, sticks and comb. The green paint was my first attempt at making a milk paint. It was not waxed and has had no intentional distressing other than the normal wear and tear of family life. It's doing well.

This commissioned chair was an adventure. I found a curved ash branch, so I was able to make my first two-part scarfed and wedged armbow. The chair has a piece of oak with character for the seat, 10 ash sticks and an ash comb, legs and stretchers. The naturally curved ash arm supports have that gnarly grain that seems to encapsulate the life of a small tree in a harsh environment. The wood was never aged. It was painted with Lexington green milk paint, with a little added black, then waxed. Nearly 20 years later, everything has mellowed to a pleasing warmth with that dry bloom look some of the old chairs have. I once heard an elderly antique furniture dealer describe this look as "sleepy." It was a pleasure to exhibit this chair at Westonbirt, The National Arboretum in Gloucestershire in "Chairs 2004."

This, and the following chairs, were made in Spencertown, N.Y.
The seat of this chair is English-grown burr oak from Picklescott,
Shropshire. Ash sticks, legs and comb. Three-part arm in hard maple. Side
stretchers and two arm posts in white oak, center stretcher hickory.

Finished with boiled linseed oil, no wax involved. I left the seat unfinished,
owing to burr wood taking up the linseed oil quite aggressively in parts. It's
coloring down well with time. It's my daughter's favorite chair.

This and the two previous chairs are known as "lobster pot" chairs.
Linseed oil and wax finish. English elm seat with ash throughout, scarfed and wedged armbow. Neither this chair nor the previous one had any wood-aging treatment. After several years, the color is getting good and mellow.

This chair, made at the start of the COVID-19 pandemic, was a major step for me down the road of getting the feeling I needed into a chair. It's the only chair I have ever pictured completely in my head, then built and finished. It seemed to flow through me. Most chairs are a journey from armbow to what is possible, and I will work through various cul-de-sacs and hiccups along the way. Not this one.

The finishing process on this chair was similar to that described in chapter one. This one was finished with homemade black milk paint. American white elm seat (extremely difficult to work – much belligerence needed). Scarfed and wedged ash armbow. This was my first North Wales four-stick-inspired chair. It owes a lot to the chair on the over of John Brown's great book, "Welsh Stick Chairs." I consider this to be the most important chair I've ever made, certainly in my understanding and development.

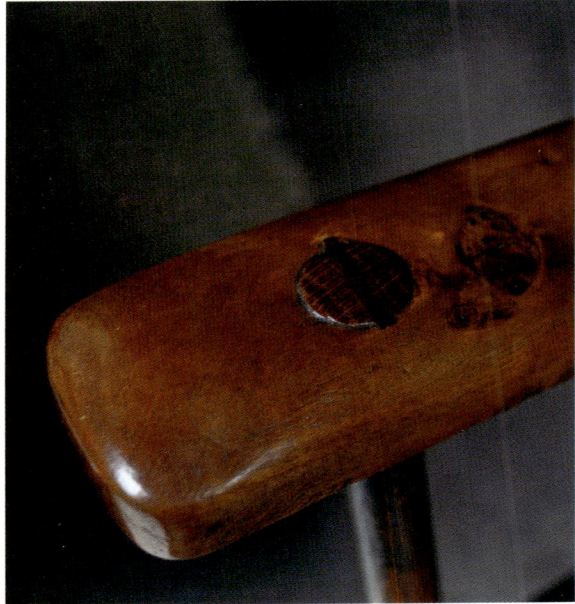

Inspired by a chair from the wonderful book "The Welsh Stick Chair" by Tim and Betsan Bowen. Finished using nitric acid, Lexington green milk paint with a little added black, shellac, cement dust, linseed oil and 10-percent roofing cement with wax. The scarfed arms are in black birch – a great wood to work and color. They were eventually burnished with heavy brown paper after the chainmail burnisher and antler. White oak seat, American white elm comb; red oak legs, stretchers and sticks.

My first attempt at working a chair in red.

Before painting, I used nitric acid, then Salem red paint, most of which I took right back off, scrubbing with coarse and medium 3M pads with thinners. After that, I painted it over with one coat of a mixture of red, brown and black milk paint. Shellac, cement dust, linseed oil, 10-percent roofing cement and wax completed the process. English elm seat, black birch two-part armbow, white oak comb. The legs, stretchers and sticks are red oak.

Soft maple two-part seat, cross-tenoned and pegged with scarfed hickory arms and sticks, oak comb, ash arm supports, legs and stretchers. Finished using nitric acid, a workshop-mixed thin brown milk paint, then shellac, cement dust, linseed oil and wax, with 10-percent roofing cement. I enjoy its stolid, "I'm here. That alright with you?" stance.

Another version of a North Wales four-stick chair. This exceedingly comfortable chair was left in the paint and waxed to allow Tom, its owner, to perform DIY chair distressing, at least three times a day. Oh yes, and let's not forget the tea breaks. American white elm two-part seat, cross-tenoned and pegged, scarfed black birch armbow, hickory sticks and legs with an ash comb.

I really enjoy the visual movement of this chair. It is entirely made of white oak, apart from the scarfed and pegged arms of ash. The chair was fumed for 72 hours with ammonia then (minus the use of vinegar iron and brown mahogany oil stain) it was worked in a similar fashion to the green chair, Backstool No. 2 in chapter two. I did over-paint a lot of the Lily Pad green to get that crusty look, which I later distressed with the chainmail burnisher.

Apart from being stung by a tiny wasp while foraging by the roadside – where I managed to find an excellent piece of white oak for the comb – this chair came together happily.

Another very comfortable red chair. The photo of the entire chair was taken right after it was made; the two detail shots are after several months of use.

Note how the workshop-mixed milk-paint surface of mulberry is chipping with use to let the thick flag-red milk paint come through. Not introduced wear. I have enjoyed watching this evolve. Better than watching paint dry. White oak seat, legs, stretchers and comb, hickory sticks, ash armbow and doubler.

This chair is now in a collection with the chair on page 81.

Over the years, I've made quite a few child's chairs. To my eye, this one works well for proportion. The paint is Lily Pad green with a coat of Lexington green over the top, cut back to let the Lily Pad come through on the seat. The wear-through to the wood on the seat front, and slight wear all around, is my suggestion of rough-and-tumble in a nursery. Soft maple cross-tenoned and pegged seat, black birch two-part scarfed and pegged arm, ash legs, stretchers and sticks. Two outer sticks red oak.

I spent a long time attempting to get the white oak seat, hickory sticks, and ash arms and doubler, legs, stretchers and comb to a satisfactory surface. It didn't work. So, over the entire chair (bar the arms) I painted Arabian Night black milk paint. Things don't always work out – I think I was pushing too hard for an effect the chair didn't need. I think this chair, which has a busy appearance, looks better for its unity of surface. This might be considered a fall-back position, but it is one I'm happy with. How much belligerence can one chair take? How much tea can one man drink?

Chemical & Glue Notes

Nitric acid is a wonderful base to build color from. It was used in the U.S. on the early maple gun stocks; it still is used today. In England, the 18th-century London cabinet firm of Coxed & Wooster used nitric, followed by a rubbing of lamp lack, maybe oil, then definitely a varnish to color their furniture sold as mulberry wood. In fact, these pieces were made of burr maple and/or burr ash veneer. Fabulous looking furniture. However, if in your own work the acid appears to deliver too strong a color, give it a coat or two of hydrogen peroxide, dry it, then neutralize it with white vinegar (a weak acetic acid). If it still seems too much, use oxalic acid with warm water, dry off, clean with warm soapy water, rinse with cold, leave for a while and reassess. Tannic acid, vinegar and iron seem less daunting and can produce wonderful, subtle effects on wood as well as oak. I want to experiment more with these, observing the effects with and without the hot air gun.

Fuming as a base with white and red oak is an excellent start to a surface. In England I used .880 ammonia and no tea washes on oak. In the U.S., I've used a 10 percent ammonia solution (with no added soap); this needs to be left for up to 72 hours. Twenty-five percent solution is harder to get but I believe it would be much quicker. On the American oaks I use a tea wash because the wood seems to have less tannic acid. **However you fume, it is astonishingly nasty stuff. Do not breathe in the fumes.** I do enjoy the clarity fuming imparts to oak. It gives a superb base to work from.

A word about glue (a sticky subject): For most of my restoration work, I use hot hide glue. I know this as Scotch glue. I nearly never use epoxy – it can push joints slightly apart during curing. And it is very hard to reverse. For my new chairs, I use the white Gorilla Glue. The main reason is that with all the disturbances in coloring the chair, I don't want to degrade a water-soluble Scotch glue. I've also observed in my time in upstate New York that the extremely damp summers and unbelievably dry, cold winters do take their toll on furniture – coupled, of course, with the heating systems in use. But each to their own. One thing I do is rough up my wedge sides to get a little more surface for the glue. I use a small, coarse rasp for this process.

Suppliers

Gary R. Wood & Co. Polishes & Supplies
Canaan, New Hampshire
http://garyrwood.com
 A very good source for finishing materials. He stocks Fiddes Mating Agent for Shellac, which I find invaluable in restoration. I mix it 80 percent shellac to 20 percent matting agent or a 90/10 ratio – it will dull down finishes. The more matting agent, the more diffuse and opaque. The 8-stick green chair in this book was made from fumed white oak. The arms in ash were aged then finished using shellac/matting agent, cement dust and pigments – invaluable.

The Real Milk Paint Co.
Hohenwald, Tennessee
https://www.realmilkpaint.com/
 I love the company's Lily Pad green. I've used it on its own, then been somewhat belligerent with it. Good reds too; these have also been adapted and occasionally mixed with blue and black.

The Old Fashioned Milk Paint Co.
Tooele, Utah
https://milkpaint.com
 I have used the company's Lexington Green on several chairs over the years, sometimes adding black, sometimes not.

Elbow Grease
At arm's length
 I think you'll know where to find it, but some perseverance will be needed. Self supplied.

About the Author

John Porritt has worked with wood since his childhood, making little boats of elder to sail on the Hampshire streams and constructing bows and arrows to play with in the woods. His initial training was at Stokecroft Arts in North London in the mid 1970s, followed by six months of carpentry instruction at the government skill center in Sittingbourne, Kent. He then attended Shrewsbury College of Arts and Technology where he studied fine furniture making with John Price (who trained with Edward Barnsley in the Arts & Crafts furniture tradition). Since 1980, Porritt has been self-employed, initially as a designer/maker then gravitating to furniture restoration, finishing and chairmaking. Having moved with his family to upstate New York in 2008, Porritt has been making his living restoring antique tools and furniture, giving talks and occasionally making a new piece. His fascination with Welsh stick chairs comes from their diversity and direct use of available materials. He loves the idea that some of these Welsh chairs feel as if they are half out of the hedge.

www.johnporrittchairs.com
Instagram: @jporrittchairs

Select Bibliography

Brian Baron, *The Techniques of Traditional Woodfinishing* (London: B.T. Batsfords Books, 1987).

Michael Bennett, *Refinishing Antique Furniture* (Leicester: Dryad Press, 1980).

Michael Bennett, *Discovering and Restoring Antique Furniture* (London: Cassell & Co., 1990).

George Frank, *Adventures in Wood Finishing* (Newtown, Connecticut: The Taunton Press, 1981).

Stan Learoyd, *The Conservation and Restoration of Antique Furniture* (New York: Sterling Publishing, 1983).

Tristan Salazar, *The Complete Book of Furniture Restoration* (New York: St. Martin's Press/Bison Books, 1982).

And look up Armand La Montagne's "Brewster Chair" – worth reading about.

Photo Credits

Pages 2, 70-71, 74, 76-91 by Lydia Curran.
https://www.monstermachineshop.net

Pages 66-69 by Graham Moss.